WALKING IN THE CLOUDS

雲中漫步

Laura

New York

Walking in the Clouds

雲中漫步

Mei Yuk Wong

黄美玉

SERENDIPITY

First published in 2002 by
Serendipity
Suite 530
37 Store Street
Bloomsbury
London

British Library Cataloguing-in-Publication data
A catalogue record for this book is available from the British Library

ISBN 1-84394-037-X

Printed and bound by Alden Press, Oxford

CONTENTS

STRUCTURAL NOTE

The Poems and Artwork section falls into two distinct catagories. Initially the photographic plates displaying the poems as they appeared in exhibition followed by the English and Chinese transcriptions as text. The page numbers quoted next to the poem title refer to the textual versions of the poems.

目 錄

註：本書的編排主要分爲兩部分，首部分的攝影形象及刺繡詩詞是在巡迴展覽時的裝置形式；第二部分則是中英文詩的並列對照。

ACKNOWLEDGEMENTS

I would like to give thanks for my family and some special friends who have given me tremendous support to publish this book and run this exhibition tour both in Hong Kong and in Manchester. They are Mrs Eleanor Ashton, Ms Alison Siu, Mr Simon Burder, Miss Model, Miss Hilary Bichovsky, Ms Rose Wu, Ms Kathy Breen, Ms Louise Wong, Ms Stella Chu, Ms Irene Pang, Ms Brony Woo, Ms Kwai Chun Lau, Hong Kong Christian Institute, Parkhurst Centre and Serendipity.

Here is my little achievement during the past year. I hope you will enjoy it and you may have your own love stories to tell and to write.

Mei Yuk Wong

鳴　謝

能夠成功出版這本書，以至在香港及英國曼徹斯特舉辦兩次個人巡迴展覽，實在有賴家人及朋友的支持。藉此我特別要感激一些好友在各方面的幫忙。他們包括Mrs. Eleanor Ashton，蕭兆滿女士， Mr. Simon Burder， Ms. Hilary Bichovsky，模特兒小姐，胡露茜女士，Ms. Kathy Breen，黃婉明女士，朱艷珊女士，黃麗玲女士，胡慕貞女士，劉貴春女士；香港基督徒學會，Pankhurst Centre及Serendipity。

我希望這些作品能帶給大家一點美麗的回憶，無論過去的感情曾受過多深的傷害，讓那些傷痕都成爲過去，使我們可以有勇氣與期盼展望將來。或許，你也有未說未寫的愛情故事有待分享。

黃美玉

PREFACE

When I visited Mei Yuk's exhibition of poems and photographs in Manchester in January 2002, it looked pale and fluid at first glance. Cotton banners hung elegantly, carrying cargoes of embroidered poems in Chinese and English. Many of the poems were accompanied by sparse, sometimes erotic, black and white photographs which are laminated onto the body of the cloth so that its weave became their grain. The poems – some of which form this book – were about love. Reading them I found a strength and honesty which reminded me of Mei Yuk herself.

I circulated greedily around the room, looking and reading – I didn't want to misss anything. Mei Yuk's own revelations released darts of emotional courage in me. Contagious – the quietly defiant act of taking down her defenses. There was something plain and pure about the way this work was offered up – the words stitched in an almost child-like way, each step of each thread holding an energy of concentration that transmitted to the reader. The expectation of love, the wait for it, the dreams of it, endure in most of us as life does – this work makes the search for love a thing of beauty.

During the January that the exhibition hung in Manchester, the US – supported by Britain – was bombing Afghanistan in revenge for the 11 September terrorist attacks. Revenge, it seemed, required no justification, was simply entitled to indulge itself. This work shines from a different facet of the human spirit. Mei Yuk is no escapist yet her poems speak of love and matters close to the heart.

I'm so glad to have the opportunity to invite you to enjoy this book.

Hilary Bichovsky
Manchester June 2002

序：人間有情

爲好友黃美玉的《雲中漫步》寫序，感到興奮之餘，亦懷著一種莫名的焦慮，因爲讀她的創作，好像在偷窺她的愛情日記。

美玉筆下的情人及背後的每一段情，都有深刻和生動的描述。從童年初戀的小子，到瀟灑博學的才俊，其中有比她年輕十多年的，亦有成熟穩重的；有單身的，亦有已成家室的；有男的，有女的；有華人，亦有不同族裔的；有愛情騙子，亦有令她依依不捨的愛人；有她不相識的露宿者，暗戀她的陌生人，亦有令她著迷，但素未謀面已逝去的人；有她尊敬和喜歡的良師，亦有她厭惡和唾棄的懦夫。

也許，有些人會覺得《雲中漫步》的黃美玉太過前衛，不夠「正經」，因爲她用情不專，到處留情。但對於我來說，讀《雲中漫步》可謂樂在其中。美玉以坦露的身體和誠實的語言，向世人剖白她過去色彩繽紛的愛情故事，是一種鼓勵和釋放。

閱讀美玉的作品，可以重新喚起我們在愛情路上曾經有過的狂想、激情、歡笑、失望、憤怒、傷痛、呼叫……等驚心動魄的回憶，縱然它們大多已被收藏在「不可見光」的密室內。

《雲中漫步》的力量就是它的磊落眞誠（即哈維爾所言的 living in truth），也因爲這種對生活光明磊落的表白，美玉這份作品更顯得珍貴動人。

衷心希望黃美玉的創作，能啓發更多人以光明磊落的精神去生活和感受生活。惟有這樣，我們才可以體會人間有情的眞、善、美。

自古以來，愛情之所以令人著迷，斷不是它的正確與否，而是在過程中所體會的人性，以及人與人在眞誠交往中的愛和關懷。

胡露茜
香港

PERSONAL STATEMENT

WHY NUDE?

To have a relationship, to love someone, you have to expose yourself in everything, just like being naked when you make love with your lover. How much can we expose ourselves to another person without keeping something or some parts of our own bodies, mind and spirit?

WHY MONOTONE?

Most of the feelings have gone. It's over. It was yesterday, the day before yesterday … I have to let go. Make the image be light and low profile, no more regret and no more hurting feelings. Let the past fantasy be black and white and gone with the wind. So that I have space and new colour for the present and the future. That is blue, the hope for being loved and to love again.

WALKING IN THE CLOUD!

Long time ago, somebody asked me what was my ideal partner? I had no clear idea. I just wanted to find someone willing to go for a walk with me every night after a meal. It is most valuable to talk with him in everything with trust. I did not mind him to be talkative, but he must have the patience to listen to my happiness and sorrowful, ups and downs.

It was my childhood daydream to walk in the cloud. Let's walk in the cloud and forget the trouble in the world, no more workload, competition, hatred, struggle for survival … but the freedom to be our own selves. To rest, to enjoy, to love the natural creation of our Mother God.

WHY BLUE EYES?

Blue eye is my answer to anybody asks my ideal boyfriend now. Why? I just like blue-eyed man. I find that man with blue eyes is very fascinating and charming. Of course, I have my 'hidden agenda'. I have been looking for a perfect man for so long. There were a lot of tears and frustration in the past. I don't want to have any more pressure from family, friends or colleagues. I was afraid of something which I didn't want to tell anybody. I need to give myself an excuse why I am so unlucky in relationships.

I know I am too fussy and I am not going to change it. So, don't bother me any more any longer! Give me a break. Never mind if in the end I will be single for the rest of my life. So what? What a big deal? I have seen many couples have arguments and troubles with their marriages and family life, including my own parents. Why should I force myself into a risk of complexity? I prefer a simple life. That is why if I recognise someone has married or even just have a girlfriend, I will stop my fancy and feelings. I hate to fall and trap into a problematic relationship.

In fact, what I demand most is not the eye colour of the man, but the honesty. He has to respect me by all means without hurting me by telling lies and having another relationship at the same time.

The monotone of yesterday has gone. I have to open for the blue, the future hope of love.

創作人的自白

爲何赤身露體？

跟一個人發生關係，愛一個人，你要把自己的全部也赤夥夥地給對方，就好像跟對方造愛時坦身露體一樣。我們究竟可以爲另一個人坦露多少？不爲自己的身體、精神與靈魂有所保留？

爲何用單一色調？

這些感情大多已成過去，是昨天的，甚至是昨天的昨天。讓這一切的舊夢如煙飛逝，好叫我爲未來預留空間，給予新的色彩。藍色，就是未來的期盼，愛與被愛的新感動。

雲中漫步

很久以前，有人問我的理想對象爲何。當時我沒有甚麼具體的想法，我只是希望有一個男子每天晚上跟我去散步，與他一起談天說地，毫無保留，眞心誠意。

兒時便有這個狂想，在雲中漫步躺臥，離開俗世的煩囂。從新拾回眞我，細心享受天上之母所創造大自然的一切。

爲何要藍眼睛？

藍眼睛就是我理想的男伴。爲甚麼？我就是覺得藍眼睛很迷人。我當然有個人的原因，只是我不想告訴任何人。從前爲尋覓愛情的路流過不少的淚，有過太多的錯折。我不想再受家人、朋友與同事的壓力，我要爲自己添個藉口。我或許要求多多，但我不打算改變條件。即使到人老朱黃仍是孤身隻影，那又何懼之有？我眼見多少夫妻反目成仇，婚姻不一定是祝福，有時反而是咒詛，那又何苦？我不會強迫自己墮入繁複的關係，我寧可抽身引退，我行我素。

其實，我最渴望遇到的不是藍眼睛，而是一個眞正對我坦誠尊重的男子。

昨天單一的調子已逝，讓我擁抱藍色，盼望未來的愛火。

Poems and Artwork: Poems at Exhibition

MEI YUK WONG

黃美玉

初戀情人
初戀多麼燦爛動人 但短暫 還記得我們
在那裡相遇 從阿姆斯特丹到倫敦的旅遊巴上
我在你的後面看着你吃奇異果
乾淨和清楚 不用匙羹或刀 因為你是紐西蘭人呢
你取笑我與身邊的華人朋友用英語對話
帶着重重的口音
我寄給你聖誕咭 因為他把我悶透了
他愚昧守舊不停地在旅程中給我麻煩
我忍受他不了
你的回音促成我們在海灘初次約會
三個月的時光我們在一起分享樂趣與熱戀
最後一次你給我一束鬱金香 我最愛的紫色
我把這束花曬乾 藏在盒子裡 保存着我倆甜蜜的回憶
初戀這麼短暫 我為你哭了三日三夜
因你突然他方遠去 先是三個月 然後是三年
使我無止境地等待
難道你不察覺 在那一夜我緊抱着你
感到我遲或早你也會遠去
我們的關係不會持久
你可知道明年是我們相識十週年
讓我們再到海灘約會吧

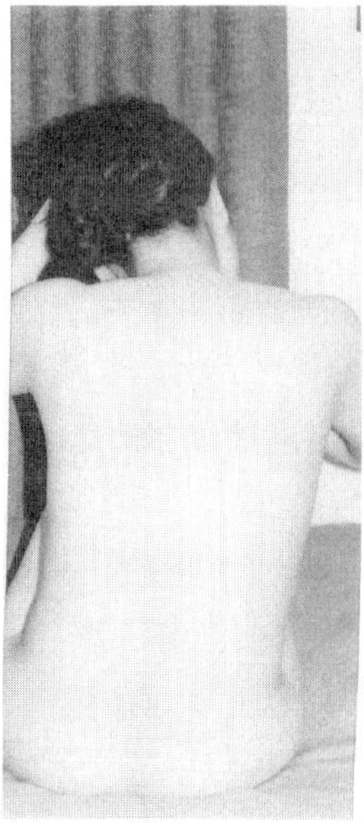

Mr Kiwi

You were my first love it was bright wild but short
do you still remember where we met
on the coach from Amsterdam to London
I sat behind you glancing at the way you ate the kiwi
very neat and clear without a spoon or knife
of course you were a kiwi
You laughed at me the way I talked to my chinese friend in English
with an accent
I sent you a christmas card for I was bored with him
he's stupid old fashioned and annoyed me a lot during the whole journey
I could bear him no more
Your response made our first date come true on th
for those three months we went out with fun and affection
the last time you gave me a bunch of tulip
it's purple my favourite I still keep those dry flowers in a tin
they remind me of our sweet memory
Why was the first love so short it made me cry for three nights and days
when I recognised you'd gone to another country
for three months and then three years I waited endlessly
Didn't you know why I was holding you so tight
I felt you would be leaving sooner or later
our relationship wouldn't last forever
Do you know next year will be our 10th anniversary
Shall we meet up for another date on the beach again

童年戀友

你的姊姊跟我青梅竹馬
她說如果我不是比你年長
我倆很合襯
其實 我比你大不了兩年
難道這是問題 真有隔膜嗎
多年以後 我們在你父親的喪禮聚首
你沒有跟我說話 我也差點認不出你來
你的妻子平凡庸俗
既沒有甚麼學位
也不是創作人才
她的樣子也不及我年輕呢
更難過的是你變得老成了
比我還成熟是生活擔子太重吧
我們真正的距離不在年齡
而是做人的態度與方向
對生命的追尋與執著
你要建立家室
而我卻在無止境地追尋
如果當初我們成了伴侶命運會否不一樣

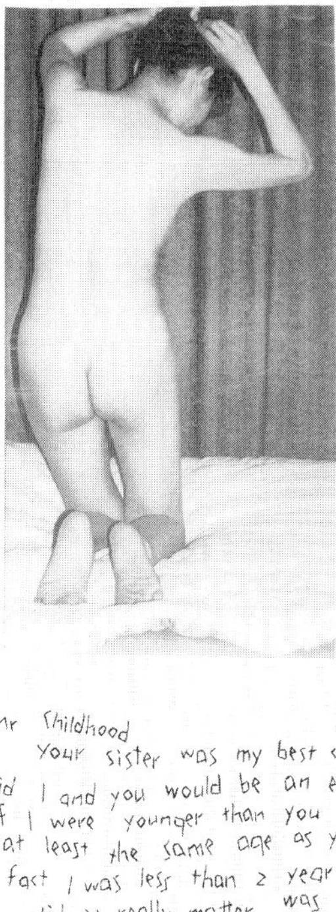

Mr Childhood
Your sister was my best childhood friend
she said I and you would be an excellent couple
only if I were younger than you
or at least the same age as you
In fact I was less than 2 years older than you
did it really matter was it a gap at all
Many years later
we met again at your father's funeral
you did not talk to me
and I'd almost totally forgotten your face
your wife looked dull
neither academic nor creative
not as young looking as I did
worse still
even you looked much older than me
too much responsibilities too many burdens
Our gap wasn't on the age
but the attitude the ambition
in searching for life's fulfilment
while you settle down with a family
I'm still struggling with my career
would there be any difference if we were a couple

花花公子

你首次出現在我眼前
只記得你好像我教會裡的一位教友
便沒有甚麼別的印象了
兩年後在我面試時你是其中一位考官
當時你沒有問過任何一個問題
否則我也未必能考入
我對你的感覺很複雜
我曾有一段時間太喜歡你了
我甚至為那個誹聞而生妒忌
傳說你與其中一名同學有婚外情呢
當我道你患了癌病時 我異常驚訝
為甚麼竟然是你 你正值壯年 又是個好人呢
當時我把個人的煩悶拋諸腦後 只為你而傷感
看見你迅速康復也為你興奮 現在的你比以前活得更痛快
時間飛逝 你已成了我的益友良師
縱然我們不會成為伴侶
但你看著我的眼神
又說我有一雙漂亮的眼睛
並欣賞我的作品
這一切我也常存心內

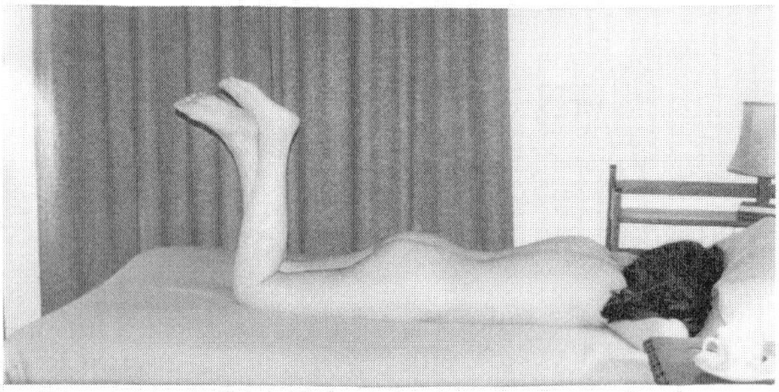

Mr Playboy

the first time we met
you looked like a guy in my church
no other special impression
Two years later
you were one of the panels
when I had the interview for my course
you did not ask a single question
otherwise I might not get in with your critical mind
My feelings for you were a complex
at some point I like you too much
that I even felt jealous when the rumour spread
you had an affair with one of the student
I was shocked knowing that you had cancer
why why you
and you just in your middle age
you were such a nice man
At that moment I forgot all my own troubles
my depression was only for you
I was glad to see you recovered so fast and so well
you lived much more happily than before
As time went by
you became my close friend
not just a favourite tutor
I knew we would never develop a relationship
By the way you looked at me
and saying that my eyes were pretty
and how much you treasured my art work
all these will keep in my mind always

情人哥哥

別人都暗說我倆在戀愛了
但你卻對我 你待我如妹妹吧?
沒有別的 就是這麼多了
對不起 我不需要多一個哥哥
我有足夠的兄弟
為何我會打破那隻杯
因為我害羞
被人問及是否喜歡你
也不知如何回答
為何你要跟我一起練琴
為何你叫我給你弄午餐
為何你要坐在我身邊看電影
他恐嚇我時 為何你那麼著緊
我甚至不是你的親妹妹 為何這麼維護我
只是你仍要否認
對我有一丁點兒的感覺
好吧 我從來不是你的情人
你也不會是我的哥哥 呢

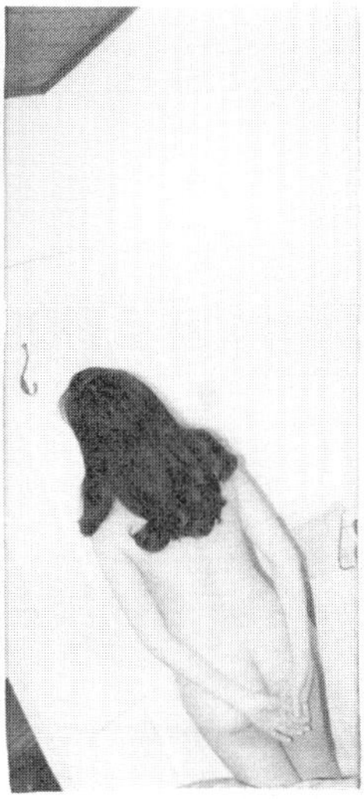

Mr Brother

Everybody said we were going out
but you told me that you treated me as your sister
nothing more and that's all
Sorry
I did not need one more brother
I got enough
How could I broke the mug
because of my shyness
to be asked if I fancy you
Why did you practise piano
why did you ask me to cook for you
why did you sit next to me in the cinema
why did you bother the crazy man threatened me
I was not even your real sister
why bother so much
Yet you still wanted to deny
as if you would never have any tiny feeling towards me
Alright then
I was not your lover
and you were never my brother too

給我手帕抹眼淚的男子
當年相識二十三歲的我
遇上四十三歲的你
被你和你的性情吸引著
雖然你的同事比你更受歡迎
那一夜在你返回故鄉前夕
你告訴我一個秘密
假如你仍是二十五歲的單身漢
你會讓我成為你的愛人 女朋友 妻子
當時我含羞塔塔
你又為我說了一個動人的愛情故事
你是王子 我是你的小公主
我保存著你給我抹眼淚的手帕
一不小心我從十六樓的家掉失了
跟著你的音訊也隨風而逝
這麼多年來我都想與你再會
跟你促膝夜談聽你的故事
可以為我再述一次那個
美麗的童話故事嗎

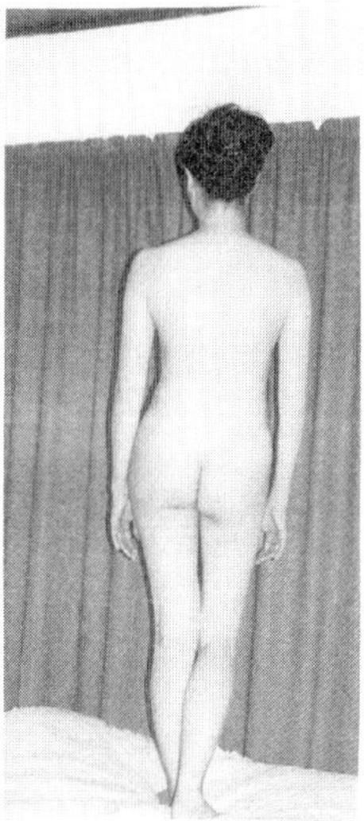

Mr Handkerchief
I was 23 and you were 43 when we first met
I liked you and your personality
even though your colleague was more popular among the group
The night before you headed off
back to your own country
you told me a secret
only if you were still single and 25
would you have me as your lover girlfriend and wife
I was so shy
and you also told me a lovely fairy tale
you were the prince
and I was your little princess
I kept your handkerchief
which you gave me when I was crying
one day I lost it from my 16th floor flat
and lost your contact later
For so many years
I have wanted to meet you again
to talk to you
to listen to your story
Will you tell me once again
the lovely fairy tale

韓國騙子
我遲到了 你是我的組長
第一個印象 你太平凡了
我開始欣賞你的領導才能
你的表達能力 你的演說技倆
我愈來愈喜歡你
但不太肯定你喜歡我還是她
給你一封情書
流露對你的傾慕
寫的是中文 我想你也明白一部分
否則你也會想辦法尋個究竟
你來訪我的城鄉時我懷著混亂的感覺
令我感到安全與心動
只是你對我的感情有多真呢
你叫我借錢給你
我猶豫了好久還是信任你
只是你和你的錢
始終也沒有回頭
為何欺騙我
我只是軟弱需要愛護
但不要說謊者

Mr Korean

I was late and
you were my group leader
you were just too ordinary
at first sight
Then I began to appreciate your leadership
your presentation
your speech
I liked you more and more
I wasn't sure if you liked me
more than her
I wrote you a letter
to show how much I adore you
but in Chinese
I supposed you understood some of it
or you'd found your way to sort it out
I had mixed feelings when you travelled to my city
I felt safe and moved
with your arm on my shoulder
but how much true feeling did you have for me in return
You asked me to lend you some money
I struggled and finally believed in you
but both the money and you
were never return never
why me
I was weak and
longing for love
but I didn't want a lier

MEI YUK WONG

黃美玉

印度懦夫

受了高等教育的你
仍未有勇氣衝破那個落後的習俗
何解又要對我表達傾慕
當我給你機會忘卻在遠方的男朋友
你便改變態度由熱轉冷
究竟有甚麼問題跟我說吧
你還要等多久
才肯擺脫那個無知的秘密
一年後我們最後一次會面
你才告訴我你要接受盲婚啞嫁
或遲或早返回故鄉
無恥啊受了高等教的你
也離不開這種落後的習俗
去吧 不要再騷擾我
你或許不還我那盒音樂帶
但我不會留下你的項鍊
以後也不想再見你
我的感情早已消逝了

Mr Indian

You were well educated
but still not brave enough
to break the stupid practice
what's the point to show me you fancy me
when I gave you a chance
to forget my boyfriend far away
you changed your mood from hot to cold
what's wrong with you
Tell me speak to me
what's the problem
for how much longer
did you intend to keep your ridiculous secret
Almost a year later when last met you
you said to fulfil your family obligation
you would have to make an arranged marriage
sooner or later back home
what a shame that
as a modern well-educated man
you still decided to follow this practice
go go go and leave me alone
You might keep my cassette
but I didn't want to keep your necklace
I'll never see you again
my feeling has gone gone gone

英俊小生
初次相見 我喜歡他勝於你
雖然你比較受歡迎
漸漸地 你跟我成了知己
你的笑容溫柔可親
你的牙齒潔白無瑕 十分悅目
我從未遇見比你更好看的男子
你的鼓勵與安慰常在我心間
伴我喜樂與煩憂
假如我是十八歲 你會讓我做你的情人
真可惜 你生得太晚了
喜歡跟你談天說地
沒有止境 也沒有沉悶
為同性戀有一致立場
跟你在一起真好 你對我很細心
也懂得欣賞我為你做的菜式
我把作品收藏在你給我的畫套內
羨慕你媽媽有這樣一個孝順兒
我希望自己也有一個像你的孩子

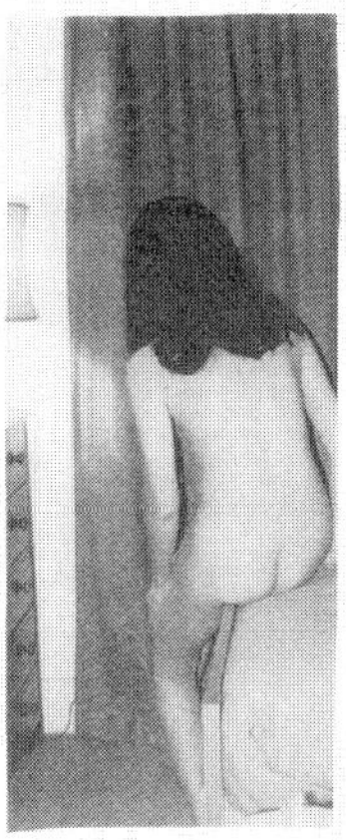

Mr Handsome
when I first met you and him
I liked him more than you
even though you were more popular
yet gradually you became closer to me
Your smile was gentle and sweet
your teeth were neat and white
just perfectly presented
and I had never seen another young man like you
Your kind words and comfort were always in my mind
both in happiness and sadness
if I were 18 you would have me as your lover
what a pity you were born just too late
enjoyed our dialogue so much
we carried on talking for ages
without boredom
even though we would never have agreement on gay issues
Our time together was precious you treated me very well
and you were delighted I cooked for you
your favourite steak
I kept my work with the portfolio that you gave me
I appreciated the way
you respected and cared for your mother
and I wish I had a son like you

獨子脾氣

我不在乎也不介意
你沒有一個學位
但你的自尊心仍是
墮得低低的
欣賞你勤奮自立
不靠父親的家財
問題出於你的脾性
獨子之故
朋友說
四十歲以後我倆若仍是單身
好應成為伴侶
我想這個絕不可能呢
可惡的你竟對我的妹妹說
我不夠漂亮來配你
我雖不是朱莉亞羅拔絲
但你也不是李察基爾呢
照照鏡看清你自己的模樣吧
你又可以配那樣的女朋友
一個從中國買來的新娘子
這又會是愛情嗎

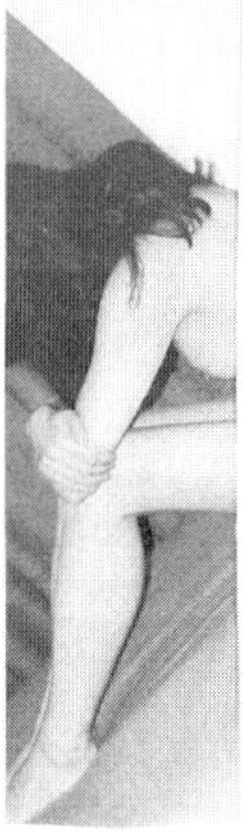

Mr Temper

I was not concerned that
you didn't have a degree
but your self esteem was still
down down down
appreciated your hard working
you didn't depend on your father or family fortune
the problem was your temper
an excuse as the only child
Some people might say
by the time we were 40 and still single
we should be a couple
I didn't think it would happen to us
How dare you told my sister that
I was not pretty enough for you
though I were not Julia Roberts
and you were not Richard Gere either
Had you ever look at yourself closely through a mirror
what kind of girlfriend did you expect
a pretty paid bride from China
but would it be true love

健康先生

無意中被你吸引
學識廣博 富幽默感 健康成熟
你還煮得一手好菜式呢
我知道你欣賞我的作品
但我不肯定你是否同樣喜歡我
每次你想要我的作品
我也會甘心情願地送給你
我曾告自己
要是一年後學成歸來
大家仍是單身的話
我會約會你呢
然而三年過去了
我沒有跟你說甚麼
我的勇氣與興趣早已消逝了
我感到一份無名的距離 你對我的了解有多深
我甚至懷疑你不會認同我的作品
讓我們繼續做普通朋友吧

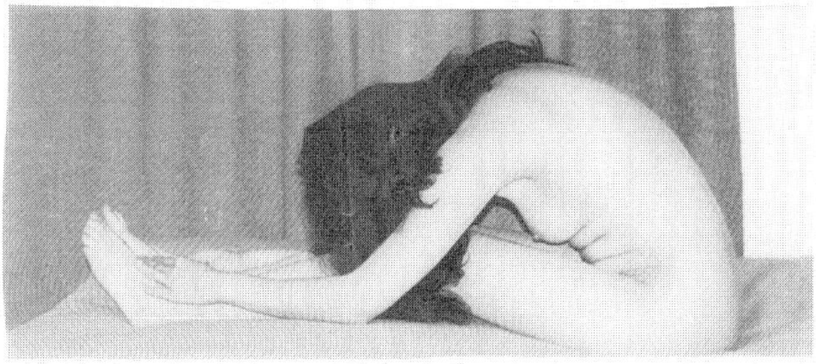

Mr Sportie
Somehow I was attracted to you
knowledgeable humarous sportie healthy mature
and you were a good cook too
I was sure you liked my work
but I wasn't sure if you liked me in the same way
whenever you asked for a piece of work
I just gave it to you naturally
I said to myself once
after I completed my course in a year's time
if both of us were still single
I would ask you for a date
well three years has gone
I never asked you for such a date
for I lost my courage and interest in the end
Somehow there was a big gap between us
I didn't think you really understand me
and not even my work
let's be friends and friends alone

香蕉先生

那隻香蕉
沒有甚麼特別意思
只是表達我的謝意 你對我的鼓勵
你給我的支持遠超過叫我寫那封投訴信
你還記得在我面試前夕
你給我肯定的說話
當藝術家不一定要有學位
你是我的精神良伴
只因你已婚又有家
否則我會爲你傾出愛意
但我怎能期待你會離婚
不 不可能
只願你有美好的前程
在北方發展你的新事業
也願有一天
我會找着像你這麼合襯的男子

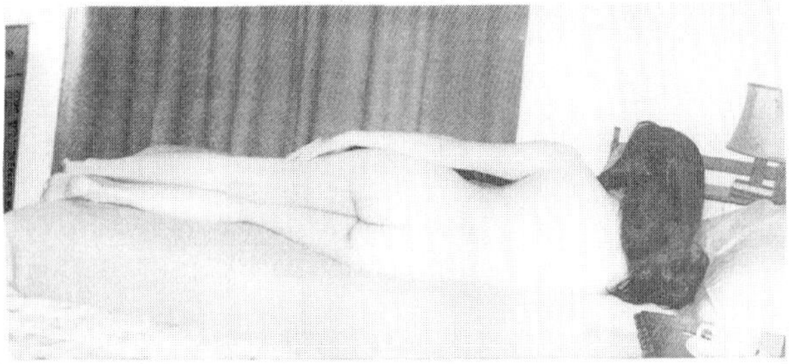

Mr Banana

The banana
nothing special
just to show my thanks
for your encouragement
You supported me so much
more than just asked me
to write a claim form
Did you remember
on the day before my interview
you reassured me
it's not necessary to have a degree
to be an artist
You were really perfect as my soul-mate
only you had get married and had a family
I would have shown my longing to be yours
how could I wish you to get a divorce
in order to have me
No it's nor possible
but all the best for your new life up north
and I hope to find someone like you
in the near future

天下第一牙刷男子

你跟你的作品同樣美妙
相識不久我已墮入你的情網裡
你的魅力無可比擬
而你對女朋友卻十分忠誠
你叫我不要再給你送禮物
我知道你已心有所屬
可是我要向她挑戰
在情人節前贏取你的心
為你編織了一條頸巾
用同樣的毛冷
為自編織了一頂帽子
我們會像情侶嗎
只是當頸巾織好時
我已失去那份勇氣
還是接受不了我倆的差異
二十五歲的你
比我的弟弟還年輕呢

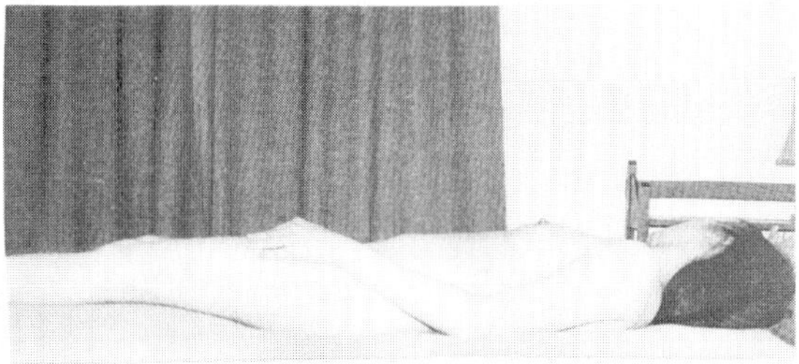

Mr Toothbrush

You are as sweet as your work
I fancy you from the very beginning
you are a nice chap and very attractive
but you are also loyal to your girlfriend
You asked me to stop giving you small gifts
I knew you had a girlfriend already
yet I wanted to challenge her
to win your heart before Valentine's Day
I knitted a scarf for you in secret
with the same wool
I knitted a hat for myself
Shall we look like a couple then
Yet when the scarf was finished
I lost my courage
I couldn't overcome the age difference
you are just 25
even younger than my brother

智慧先生

我欣賞你和你的作品
知識豐富 誠真 簡潔 尊重
當我煩惱不知如何創作
你給我亮光
使我敢於開拓其他可能
另覓出路
我喜歡你的笑容
你凝望我的眼神
令我想起那個花花公子
你的作品意念豐富
內裡隱藏着無比的力量
盼望我的作品也有這一天的功力
你的名氣
未必如畢加索
但你是我的導師
偉大的導航者

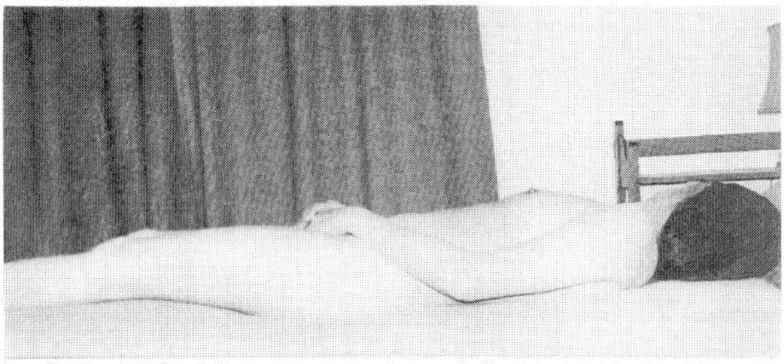

Mr Wise

I admired you and your work
knowledgeable sincere simple dignified
Whenever I was stuck with my work
you gave me insights
encouraged me to explore another possibility
the way for alternatives
I like your smile
I liked the way you looked at me
just liked Mr Playboy
The meaning behind your work was so rich
the power underneath was so great
that's what I wanted to
achieve one day
Though you might not be as famous
as Picasso
you were my great tutor
my great tutor indeed

給她送康乃馨的男子
誰令我苦惱煩心 哭泣不斷
正是你 傷透我心的人
我害怕讓你知道我對你的傾慕
為你送上一份生日禮物
用雙手編織也不知花了多少個日與夜
換來的是你十分細膩的婉拒
你害怕我喜歡你太深
你說不出為何我們不可能發展
我也說不盡何解我這麼喜歡你
在你面前我強忍著淚 往後我情不自禁
獨自在車上淚水湧流 夜深了仍戴上太陽鏡
只是要隱藏自己的感情不讓陌生人發覺
我們曾一起看展覽 晚膳 跳舞 交換電郵 賀咭
最重要的是你買了我的畫作
這一切都變得不打緊 沒有意思了
當然會把自己的感情轉易
為我的創作 為我的朋友與家人
但不會是你
我不想令你驚怕
也不想再為你受傷

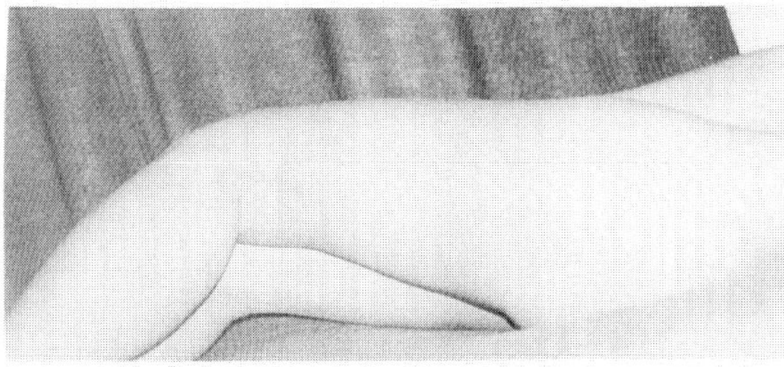

Mr Carnation
Who has ever annoyed me
and made me cry so much
it's you and it hurts
I was so scared to show my fancy to you
by giving you a birthday gift which I made
for how many days and nights
In return you refused me in a very sophisticated way
you were afraid that I liked you too much
you could not tell me why you felt it wouldn't work
and I could not explain either why I liked you so much
I controlled my tears before you then I could control it no more
tears dropped naturally when I sat down on the train alone
I still wore my sunglasses even though it was at night
trying to hide my sadness in front of strangers
we went out to see an exhibition to have a meal to dance
to exchange emails and greeting cards
and most of all you bought my paintings
but all became nothing and meaningless
Surely I'll channel my emotions
to my work
to my friends and family
but not you anymore
I don't want to scare you and
to be hurt again

暗戀我的男子
被暗戀的感覺
真的很舒服妙不可言
我所暗戀的男子
卻沒有一個滿足我的期盼
這些觀眾都欣賞我的作品
其一位還約會我呢
我要給他正面的回應
何不多認識一位新朋友 一位暗戀者
多了一個選擇
肯定地我會告訴康乃馨先生
有人暗戀我
至少可以談出他的反應
叫他妒忌
是啊如果他真的喜歡我
該多著緊些呢
這個陌生人
他凝望我的眼神
流露著
一份欣賞與暗戀之情

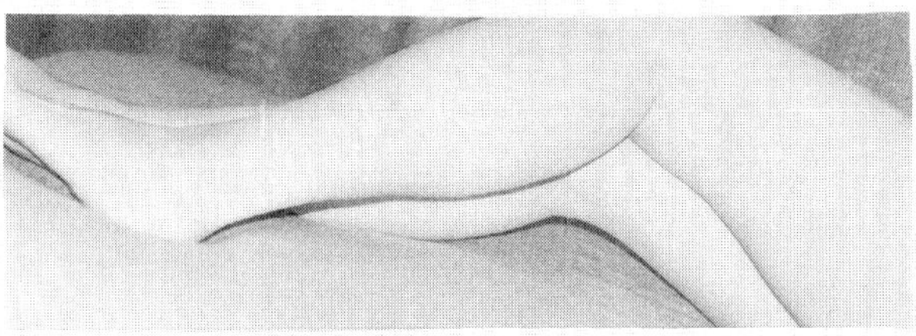

Mr Admirer
The feeling of being admired in secret
is so good and wonderful
I admire a couple of nice chaps
but none of them respond the way that I hope
Those viewers admired my work
then there was one who asked me to go for a drink
I was very positive why not
to have a new friend an admirer
to have more choices
certainly I'll tell Mr Carnation
somebody's interested in me
at least I can see how he reacts
make him jealous
yeah if he really likes me
he should be more aggressive
This stranger
the way he looked at me
there's something more inside his eyes
adoration of my work and me

慷慨小子
你對我真的好
我也喜歡你
只是你太年輕了
多麼渴望此刻的你
就是三十多歲
你給我很多小禮物
多麼慷慨
多麼富心思
你的表現比你的年齡
成熟多了
謝謝你
手牽手陪著我走泰吾時河畔
縱然不是情侶
但也是交心的良伴
爲我造一個模型
一個小小的我
在你眼裡
究竟我是怎麼樣的呢

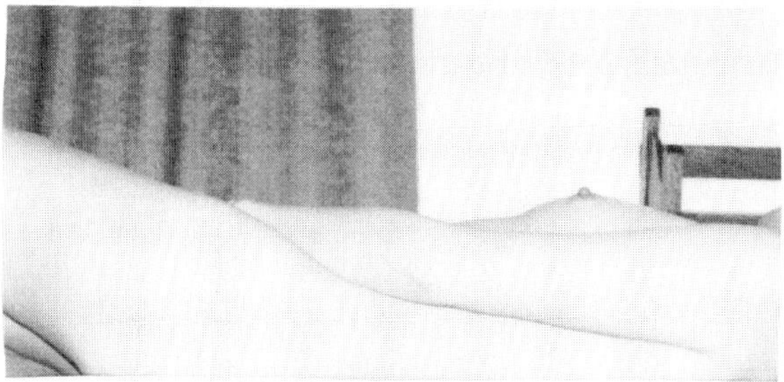

Mr Generous
You are so nice to me
I like you a lot indeed
but you are too young for me
I want you to be 3o something
right now
You have given me a lot of gifts
very generous
very thoughtful
your behaviour is very mature
for your age
Thanks for walking with me
along the River Thames
hand in hand
even though we are not a couple
but very close friends
You are going to make a model
a reflection of me
through your eyes
how will it be

怎麼愛上一個逝去的男子
保羅她的愛兒
俊俏有為惜英年早逝
愈是知道你的故事愈加深我對你的感覺
偷偷地喜歡你
我怎能告訴別人我愛上一個逝去的男子
怎麼可能我倆從未相見
只憑你的玉照我墮入你的情網
如何用筆墨形容 魅力太深
不獨是你的善良與溫柔
而是從你心內流露出的真面目
誰敢取你的性命 是那暴風雨
太詭秘了
誰能忍受失去一個年青有為
像你這樣的男子
受身邊朋友尊崇
被父母與妹妹痛愛
我奈不住
那份引誘
取一張你的玉照
可是
會否令你的母親不快

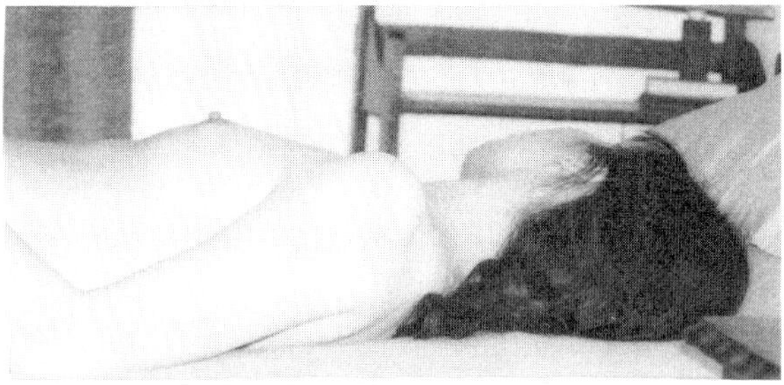

How can I fall in love with a dead young man
Paul her beloved son
handsome but dying too young
the more I get to know your story
the deeper is my feeling towards you
but in secret
how can I tell anybody I fell in love with a dead man
How can it be
we never met
just by seeing your picture
I fall in love with you
how can I put it into words
so attractive
not just because of your sweetness and gentleness
but the persona within your heart and exposed on your face
How could anyone dare to take your life
was it the storm
such a mystery
who can bear to lose a handsome young man
like you
befriended by the people around you
belove by your parents and sister
I can't resist
the temptation
to get a copy of your picture
but
will it upset your mother

怎麼為女人動情
從沒想過會愛上一個女人
印象中只有兩次轉瞬即逝的遐想
我躺在椅子上 綠小姐坐在我的身旁
突然間我被她吸引著 很想觸摸她的身軀
但這個感覺並不持久 只是幾分鐘 甚至是數秒間而已
另一次也相近 崇拜後我跟紅小姐交談
她穿了一件紅色的外套 紅得像她的臉一般明媚
她的臉皮十分單薄
她跟我說話時把我迷住了
叫我心神不定
同樣又是一剎那間的感覺
一次我跟靚仔小生辯論同性戀問題
鬧得不可開交
面紅耳熱
誰也不肯讓步
最後我問他 究竟你愛一個人
還是她/他的性器官
為何我們這麼著緊別人的性向
而不是她/他們的性情
雖然我仍然鍾情於男子
但是我也不斷提醒自己
要開放及尊重別人的性取向

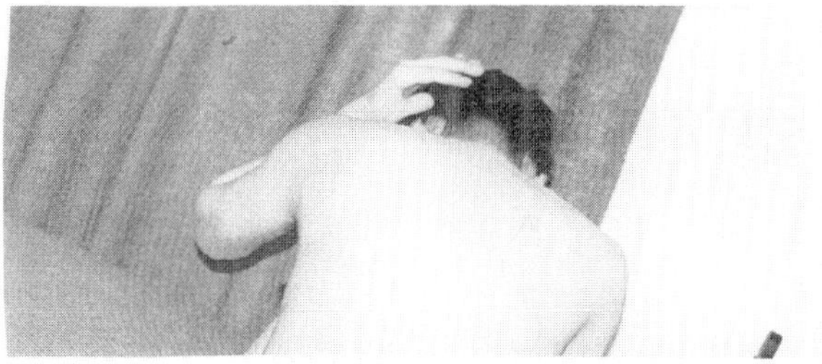

Miss Green and Miss Red
I never thought I would fall in love with a woman
Only twice and then for a very short moment
I was lying on the sofa Miss Green was sitting next to me
Suddenly I was attracted to her
I wanted to touch her body
but the emotion didn't last for long
maybe just a few minutes or even a few seconds
The other time was similar
I was talking with Miss Red after the service
she was wearing a red jacket it was as red as her face
she had very thin skin she was chatting with me
and I had the feeling for her she looked so charming
Again it didn't last long
Once I was arguing with Mr Handsome
he disagreed very much on gay issues
I was very critical too
it was impossible to have any consensus
finally I challenged him
what do you fall in love with
a person or her / his sex organ
So why do we bother so much about their sexuality
but not their personality
Though I'm still straight at the moment
I always remind myself to be open
and respect other people's different
sexual orientation

真漢子

爲何他這樣沉默
好像背負了一國的擔子
甚至是全世界的包袱
他是彌賽亞
爲何他不能享受與漂亮的女子在一起
他愚不可及還是男同志
他的傲慢難於啓齒
內心真情 爲這女子
深深地愛著 久久地等待
傲慢與偏見攔阻他公開地 自由地宣愛
然而他勇敢地尋求辦法
承認一己的錯失
一個能爲自己悔過的男子
主動爲他人做一些補救功夫
甚至不爲人道
怪不得到最終
他還是漸漸地贏取了她的心
其實
我也在追尋這樣的
真漢子

Mr Pride

Why was he so quiet
he seemed to bear the burden of
the whole nation or even of the whole world
was he the Messiah
Why couldn't he enjoy the happiness
being with the pretty woman
why was he so stupid
was he too proud to express was he gay
his true feeling for the woman
he loved so deeply in heart
for such a long time
the prides and prejudices
avoided him to love
with his free will openly
Yet
he was brave enough
to sort out
what he had done wrongly
A man can correct his fault
by doing something good for others
even in a secret manner
No wonder at the end
he won her love gradually
in fact I'm longing for such a real man too

露宿者
差不多每次我到圖書館
他都站在大門口兜售大件事
我跟他有何分別大家都很辛勤地工作
究竟他可以賣出多少本
不論春夏秋冬就是每天站著七小時
他住在那兒受過教育沒有
還有其他工作嗎為何成了露宿者
我不知他的名字
每次只是點頭打聲招呼
他也微笑地跟我說聲好
我想多認識他嗎
更個人的而不是其中一名露宿者
突然間我發覺他的藍眼睛
我是否已被他吸引了
怎麼會這樣
他沒有工作沒有棲身之所沒有錢
他甚麼也沒有
但他是個好人
有一臉溫柔的性情
從他善良的心而出

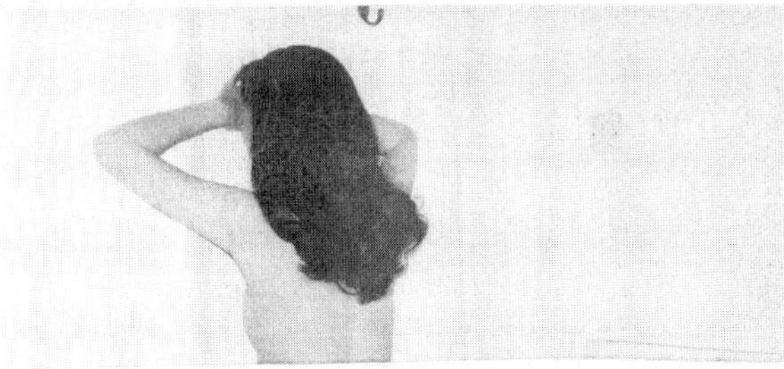

Mr Homeless
Almost every time I go to the library
he stands in front of the entrance
selling Big Issue for a living
what's the difference between him and me
we both work very hard
I wonder how many copies does he sell
for standing 7 hours a day both in summer and in winter
where does he live
does he have any education
does he have another job
what made him become homeless
I don't know his name
I just say hi or good morning to him
and he says hi or smiles to me too
Do I want to know him more in person
not just one of the homeless
suddenly I recognised he had blue eyes
am I attracted to him
How could it be
he has no job no place to live no money
he has nothing
yet he looks a nice person
with sweet personality from within his heart

藍眼睛

我愛藍眼睛的男子 我只愛藍眼睛的他
我的男人 我的丈夫 我的伴侶
怎樣稱呼他也不相干 也不打緊
不介意我的男人離了婚或已喪偶
或是裝修工人 甚至是非基督徒
但他必然要誠懇地愛我
好像透明的花瓶般真摯
我想有一個孩子 為他命名叫雨果
不宜當高齡產婦 但我可收養一個孩子
這麼多的孤兒期待着擁抱
無條件的愛 溫暖又安全的家
何解偏偏要自己生的孩子
我會心滿意足
如果他同意收養一個孩子
或是給我帶來一個
愛一個藍眼睛的男人
有一個收養的孩子

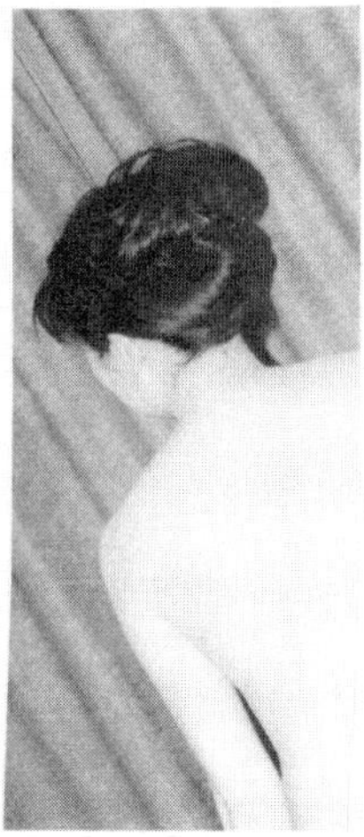

Blue-eyes

I love the man with blue eyes
I like blue eyes and blue eyes only
My man my husband my partner
it doesn't matter how to call him
I don't mind if my man is a divorcee
a widower builder a non-christian
but he must love me truly with
honesty just like a stransparent vase
I want to have a child and his name
will be Hugo
too old for a first baby
Too many children are waiting for a big hug
an unconditional love a warm and safe home
why bother to have my own baby
I'll be contented
if he agrees to adopt a child
or bring me one
have a blue-eyed man and
get a child for free

Poems and Artwork: Poems in English and Chinese

A WALK IN THE CLOUDS

A walk in the clouds
away from the crowd

This is my childhood day dream
to walk softly
to lie comfortably
on top of the clouds
high up into the sky

What a clever idea
What a wonderful feeling
much better than swimming in the sea

The sky is blue and clear
the cloud is white and pure

There is no more trouble
no more burden
no more homework
no more argument
no more fighting
no more noise
no more pollution …
away from all the earthly matter

When will this dream come true
like a fairy tale
only if I were a character in an animation!
Harry Potter?

(in *A Voyage into Fantasy* by Anchor Books, p. 74, 2001)

雲中漫步

雲中漫步
遠離凡塵

兒時狂想
雲中漫步
躺於雲端
超越高崇的天空

多麼聰明的遐想
多麼爽快的感覺
比在海中暢泳更新鮮

天空蔚藍皎潔
雲兒潔白無瑕

在那裡再沒有煩惱
沒有擔子
沒有功課
沒有爭拗
沒有打鬥
沒有囂鬧
沒有污染
遠離一切凡塵俗世，是是非非

甚麼時候這個夢想成真
好像童話故事
待我成了動畫的主角！
哈利波特？

MR KIWI

You were my first love
it was bright, wild but short
do you still remember where we met
on the coach from Amsterdam to London

I sat behind you
glancing at the way you ate the kiwi
very neat and clear without a spoon or knife
of course you were a Kiwi

You laughed at me
the way I talked to my Chinese friend in English
with an accent

I sent you a Christmas card
for I was bored with him
he's stupid, old fashioned
and annoyed me a lot during the whole journey
I could bear him no more

Your response made our first date come true on the beach
for those three months,
we went out, with fun and affection

The last time you gave me a bunch of tulip
it's purple, my favourite
I still keep those dry flowers in a tin
they remind me of our sweet memory

Why was the first love so short?
It made me cry for three nights and days
when I recognised you'd gone to another country
for three months and then three years
I waited endlessly

Didn't you know why I was holding you so tight
I felt you would be leaving
sooner or later
our relationship wouldn't last forever

Do you know next year will be our 10th anniversary
Shall we meet up for another date on the beach again?

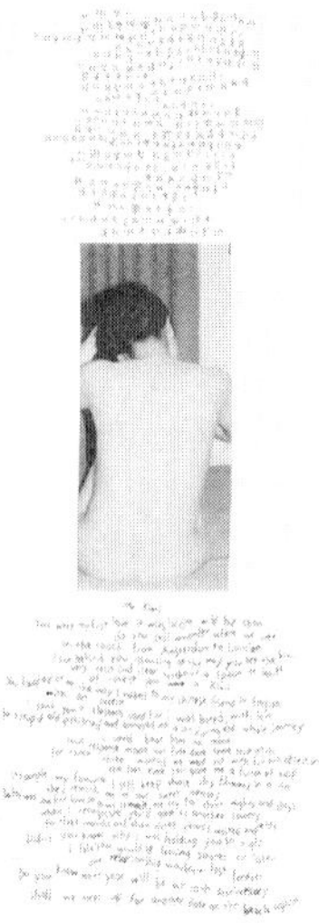

初戀情人

初戀多麼燦爛、野性，但短暫
還記得我們在那兒相遇
從阿姆斯特丹到倫敦的旅遊巴上

我坐在你的後面
看著你吃奇異果
乾淨利落不用匙羹或刀
因爲你是紐西蘭人呢

你取笑我
跟身邊的華人朋友用英語對話
帶著重重的口音

給你寫聖誕咭
因爲他把我悶透了
他愚昧守舊
不停地在旅途中給我麻煩
我忍受他不了

你的回音促成我們在海灘初次約會
三個月的時光
我們在一起分享樂趣與熱戀

最後一次你給我一束鬱金香
我最愛的紫色
我把這束花晒乾藏在盒子裡
保存著我倆甜蜜的回憶

初戀這麼短暫
我爲你哭了三日三夜
因你突然他方遠去
先是三個月，然後是三年
使我無止境地等待

難道你不察覺
在那一夜我緊抱著你
感到或遲或早你也會遠去
我們的關係不會持久

你可知道明年是我們相識十週年
讓我們再到海灘約會吧！

MR CHILDHOOD

Your sister was my best childhood friend
she said, I and you would be an excellent couple
only if I were younger than you
or at least the same age as you

In fact,
I was less than 2 years older than you
did it really matter
was it a gap at all?

Many years later
we met again at your father's funeral
you did not talk to me
and I'd almost totally forgotten your face

Your wife looked dull
neither academic nor creative
not as young looking as I did

worse still
even you looked much older than me
too much responsibilities
too many burdens?

Our gap wasn't on the age
but the attitude, the ambition,
in searching for life's fulfilment
while you settle down with a family
I'm still struggling with my career

Would there be any difference if we were a couple?

童年戀友

你的姊姊跟我青梅竹馬
她說如果我不是比你年長
我倆很合襯

其實
我比你大不了兩年
難道這是問題
真有隔膜嗎？

多年以後
我們在你父親的喪禮聚首
你沒有跟我說話
我也差點認不出你來

你的妻子平凡庸俗
既沒有甚麼學位也不是創作人才
她的樣子也不及我年輕呢！

更難過的是
你變得老成了
比我還成熟
是生活擔子太重吧？

我們真正的距離不在年齡
而是做人的態度與方向
對生命的追尋與執著
你要建立家室
而我卻在無止境地追尋

如果當初我們成了伴侶命運會否不一樣？

MR PLAYBOY

The first time we met
you looked like a guy in my church
no other special impression

Two years' later
you were one of the panels
when I had the interview for my course
you did not ask a single question
otherwise I might not get in with your critical mind

My feelings for you were a complex
at some point I liked you too much
I even felt jealous when the rumour spread
that you had an affair with one of the students!

I was shocked knowing that you had cancer
Why, why you?
you were just in your middle age
and you were such a nice man

At that moment I forgot all my own troubles
my depression was only for you
I was glad to see you recovered so fast and so well
you lived much more happily than before

As time went by
you became my close friend
not just a favourite tutor
I knew we would never develop a relationship

By the way you looked at me
and saying that my eyes were pretty
and how much you treasured my art work …
all these will keep in my mind always

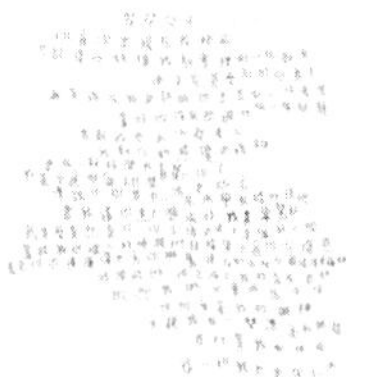

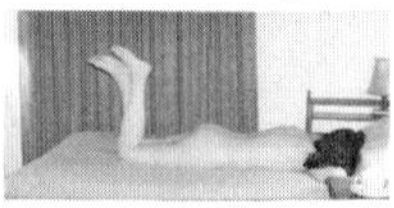

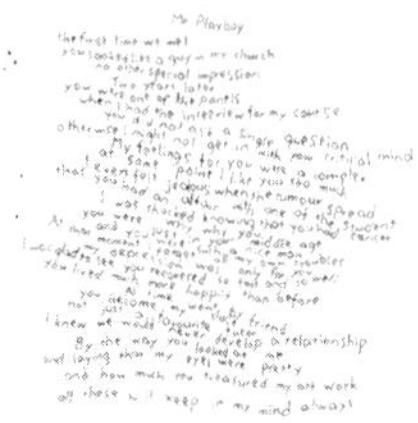

花花公子

你首次出現在我眼前
只記得你好像我教會裡的一位教友
便沒有甚麼別的印象了

兩年後在我面試時
你是其中一位考官
當時你沒有問過任何一個問題
否則我也未必能考入

我對你的感覺很複雜
曾有一段時間太喜歡你了
我甚至爲那個緋聞而生妒忌
傳說你與其中一名同學有婚外情呢！

當我知道你患了癌病時
我異常驚訝
爲甚麼竟然是你？
你正值中年
又是個好人呢！

當時我把個人的煩悶拋諸腦後
只爲你而傷感
看見你迅速康復也爲你興奮
現在的你比以前活得更痛快

時間飛逝
你已成了我的益友
不獨是良師
縱然我們不會成爲伴侶

但你看著我的眼神
又說我有一雙漂亮的眼睛
並欣賞我的作品
這一切我也常存心內

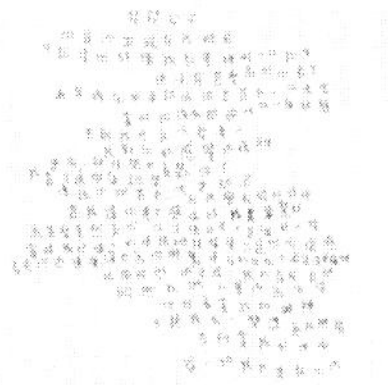

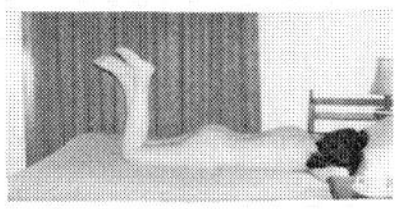

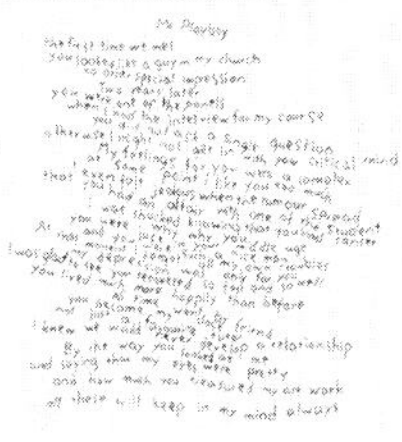

MR BROTHER

Everybody wondered we were going out together
but you told me that you just treated me as your sister
nothing more
and that's all

Sorry,
I did not need one more brother
I got enough

How could I broke the mug
because of my shyness
being asked if I fancy you

Why did you practise piano with me
why did you ask me to cook for you
why did you sit next to me in the cinema
why did you bother the crazy man threatened me

I was not even you real sister
why bother so much

Yet you still wanted to deny
as if
you would never have any tiny feeling towards me

Alright then,
I was not your lover
and you were never my brother too!

情人哥哥

別人都暗說我倆在戀愛了
但你卻對我說你待我如妹妹吧了
沒有別的
就是這麼多了

對不起
我不需要多一個哥哥
我有足夠的兄弟

爲何我會打破那隻杯
因爲我害羞
被人問及是否喜歡你
也不知如何回答

爲何你要跟我一起練琴
爲何你叫我給你弄午餐
爲何你要坐在我身邊看電影
他恐嚇我時爲何你那麼著緊

我甚至不是你的親妹妹
爲何這麼維護我

只是你仍要否認
對我曾有一丁點兒的感覺

好吧
我從來不是你的情人
你也不會是我的哥哥呢！

MR HANDKERCHIEF

I was 23 and you were 43 when we first met
I liked you and your personality
even though your colleague was more popular
among the group

The night before you headed off
back to your own country
you told me a secret
only if you were still single and 25
would you have me as your lover, girlfriend and wife

I was so shy
and you also told me a lovely fairy tale
you were the prince
and I was your little princess …

I kept your handkerchief
which you gave me when I was crying?
one day I lost it from my 16th floor flat
and I lost your contact later

For so many years
I have wanted to meet you again
to talk to you
to listen to your story

Will you tell me once again the lovely fairy tale?

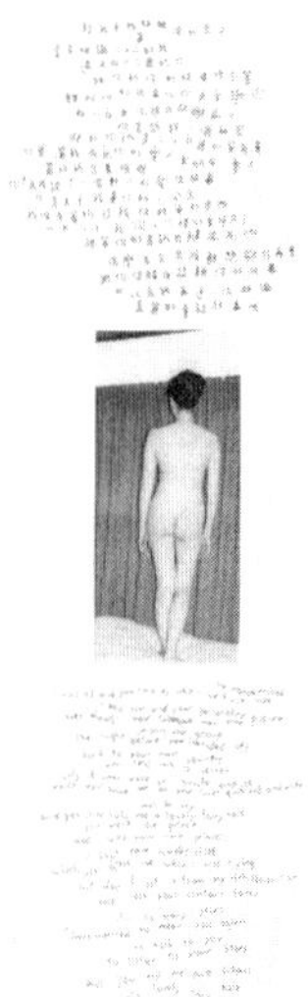

(In *Poetic Thoughts* by *Poetry Now*, p. 48, 2002)

給我手帕抹眼淚的男子

當年相識
二十三歲的我遇上四十三歲的你
被你和你的性情吸引著
雖然你的同事比你更受歡迎

那一夜
在你返回故鄉前夕
你告訴我一個秘密
假如你仍是二十五歲的單身漢
你會讓我成爲你的愛人，女朋友，妻子

當時我含羞答答
你又爲我說了一個動人的愛情故事
你是王子
我是你的小公主

我保存著
你給我抹眼淚的手帕
一不小心我從十六樓的家掉失了
跟著你的音訊也隨風而逝

這麼多年來
我都想與你再會
跟你促膝夜談
聽你的故事

可以爲我再述一次那個美麗的童話故事嗎？

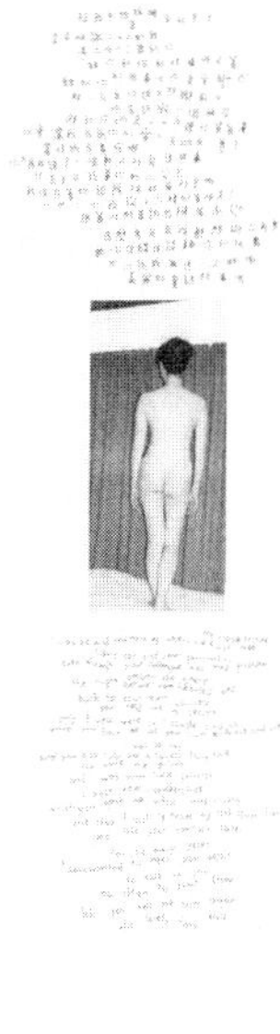

MR KOREAN

I was late and
you were my group leader
you were just too ordinary
at first sight

Then I began to appreciate your leadership
your presentation
your speech
I liked you more and more

I wasn't sure if you liked me
more than her
I wrote you a letter
to show how much I adore you

but in Chinese
I supposed you understood some of it
or you'd found your way to sort it out

I had mixed feelings when you travelled to my city
I felt safe and moved
with your arm on my shoulder
but how much true feeling did you have for me in return?

You asked me to lend you some money
I struggled and finally believed in you
but both the money and you
were never return, never!

Why me?
I was weak and
longing for love
but I didn't want a liar!

韓國騙子

我遲到了
你是我的組長
第一個印象
你太平凡了

我開始欣賞你的領導才能
你的表達能力
你的演說技倆
我愈來愈喜歡你

但不太肯定你喜歡我
還是她
給你一封情書
流露對你的傾慕

寫的是中文
我想你也明白一部分
否則你也會想辦法尋個究竟

你來訪我的城鄉時
我懷著混亂的感覺
你的手臂放在我肩上
令我感到安全與心動
只是你對我的感情有多真呢？

你叫我借錢給你
我猶豫了好久還是信任你
只是你和你的錢
始終也沒有回頭！

爲何欺騙我？
我只是軟弱
需要愛護
但不要說謊者！

MR INDIAN

You were well-educated
but still not brave enough
to break the stupid practice
what's the point to show me you fancy me

When I gave you a chance
to forget my boyfriend far away
you changed your mood from hot to cold
what's wrong with you

Tell me, speak to me
what's the problem
for how much longer
did you intend to keep your ridiculous secret?

Almost a year later when I last met you
you said, to fulfil your family obligation
you would have to make an arranged marriage
sooner or later back home

What a shame that,
as a modern, well-educated man
you still decided to follow this practice
go, go, go and leave me alone!

You might keep my cassette
but I didn't want to keep your necklace
I'll never see you again
my feeling has gone, gone, gone

印度懦夫

受了高等教育的你
仍未有勇氣
衝破那個落後的習俗
何解又要對我表達傾慕

當我給你機會
忘卻在遠方的男朋友
你便改變態度由熱轉冷
究竟有甚麼問題？

跟我說吧
問題在那裡
你還要等多久
才肯擺脫那個無知的秘密？

一年後我們最後一次會面
你才告訴我
你要接受盲婚啞嫁
或遲或早返回故鄉

無恥啊
受了高等教育的你
也離不開這種落後的習俗
去吧，不要再騷擾我

你或許不還我那盒音樂帶
但我不會留下你的項鍊
以後也不想再見你
我的感情早已消逝了

MR HANDSOME

When I first met you and him
I liked him more than you
even though you were more popular
yet, gradually you became closer to me

Your smile was gentle and sweet
your teeth were neat and white
just perfectly presented
and I had never seen another young man like you

Your kind words and comfort
were always in my mind
both in happiness and sadness

If I were 18,
you would have me as your lover
what a pity
you were born just too **late**!

I enjoyed our dialogue so much
we carried on talking for ages
without boredom
even though we would never have agreement
on gay issues

Our time together was precious
you treated me very well
and you were delighted I cooked for you
your favourite steak
I kept my work with the portfolio that you gave me

I appreciated the way
you respected and cared for your mother
and I wish I had a son like you.

英俊小生

初次相見
我喜歡他勝於你
雖然你比較受歡迎
漸漸地，你跟我成了知己

你的笑容溫柔可親
你的牙齒潔白無瑕
十分悅目
我從未遇見比你更好看的男子

你的鼓勵與安慰
常在我心間
伴我喜樂與煩憂

假如我是十八歲
你會讓我做你的情人
眞可惜
你生得太晚了！

喜歡跟你談天說地
沒有止境
也沒有沉悶
即使我們永遠不會爲同性戀
有一致立場

跟你在一起眞好
你對我很細心
也懂得欣賞我爲你做的菜式
我把作品收藏在你給我的畫套內

善慕你媽媽有這樣一個孝順兒
我希望自己也有一個像你的孩子

MR TEMPER

I was not concerned that
you didn't have a degree
but your self-esteem was still
down, down, down

I appreciated your hard working
you didn't depend on your father or family fortune
the problem was your temper
an excuse as the only child?

Some people might say
by the time we were 40 and still single
we should be a couple …
I didn't think it would happen to us!

How dare you told my sister that
I was not pretty enough for you
though I were not Julia Roberts
and you were not Richard Gere either

Had you ever look at yourself closely through a mirror?
what kind of girlfriend did you expect?
a pretty paid bride from China?
but would it be true love!

獨子脾氣

我不在乎也不介意
你沒有一個學位
但你的自尊心仍是
墮得低低的

欣賞你勤奮自立
不靠父親的家財
問題出於你的脾性
獨子之故？

朋友說
四十歲以後我倆若仍是單身
好應成爲伴侶
我想這個絕不可能呢！

可惡的你竟對我的妹妹說
我不夠漂亮來配你
我雖不是朱莉亞羅拔絲
但你也不是李察基爾呢！

照照鏡看清你自己的模樣吧
你又可以配那樣的女朋友?
一個從中國買來的新娘子
這又會是愛情嗎！

MR SPORTIE

Somehow I was attracted to you
knowledgeable,
humorous,
sportie,
healthy,
mature …
and you were a good cook too!

I was sure you liked my work
but I wasn't sure if you liked me in the same way
whenever you asked for a piece of work
I just gave it to you naturally

I said to myself once
after I completed my course in a year's time
if both of us were still single
I would ask you for a date!

Well
three years has gone,
I never asked you for such a date
for I lost my courage and interest in the end

Somehow there was a big gap between us
I didn't think you really understand me
and not even my work
let's be friends and friends alone

健康先生

無意中被你吸引
學識廣博
富幽默感
健康
成熟
你還煮得一手好菜式呢！

我知道你欣賞我的作品
但我不肯定你是否同樣喜歡我
每次你想要我的作品
我也會甘心情願地送給你

我曾告訴自己
要是一年後學成歸來
大家仍是單身的話
我會約會你呢！

然而
三年過去了
我沒有跟你說甚麼
我的勇氣與興趣早已消逝了

我感到一份無名的距離
你對我的了解有多深
我甚至懷疑你不會認同我的作品
讓我們繼續做普通朋友吧

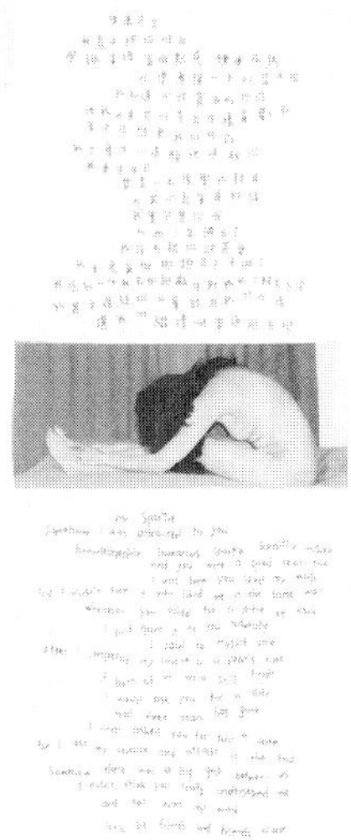

MR BANANA

The banana?
nothing special
just to show my thanks
for your encouragement

You supported me so much
more than just asked me
to write a claim form

Did you remember
on the day before my interview
you reassured me
'it's not necessary to have a degree to be an artist'

You were really perfect as my soul-mate
only you had got married and had a family
I would have shown my longing to be yours
how could I wish you to get a divorce in order to have me?

No, it's not possible
but all the best for your new life up north
and I hope to find someone like you
in the near future

香蕉先生

那隻香蕉？
沒有甚麼特別意思
只是表達我的謝意
你對我的鼓勵

你給我的支持
遠超過叫我寫那封投訴信

你還記得
在我面試前夕
你給我肯定的說話
「當藝術家不一定要有學位」

你是我的精神良伴
只因你已婚又有家室
否則我會爲你傾出愛意
但我怎能期待你會離婚？

不，不可能
只願你有美好的前程
在北方發展你的新事業
也願一天
我會找著像你這麼合襯的男子

MR TOOTHBRUSH

You were as sweet as your work
I fancy you from the very beginning
you were a nice chap and very attractive
but you are also loyal to your girlfriend

You asked me to stop giving you small gifts
I knew you had a girlfriend already
yet, I wanted to challenge her
to **win** your heart before Valentine's Day!

I knitted a scarf for you in secret
with the same wool
I knitted a hat for myself
Shall we look like a couple then?

Yet, when the scarf was finished
I lost my courage
I couldn't overcome the age difference
you were just 25
even younger than my brother!

天下第一牙刷男子

你跟你的作品同樣美妙
相識不久我已墮入你的情網裡
你的魅力無可比爾
而你對女朋友卻十分忠誠

你叫我不要再給你送禮物
我知道你已心有所屬
可是我要向她挑戰
在情人節前贏取你的心！

爲你編織了一條項巾
用同樣的毛冷
爲自己編織了一頂帽子
我們會像情侶嗎？

只是當項巾織好時
我已失去那份勇氣
還是接受不了我倆的差異
二十五歲的你
比我的弟弟還年輕呢！

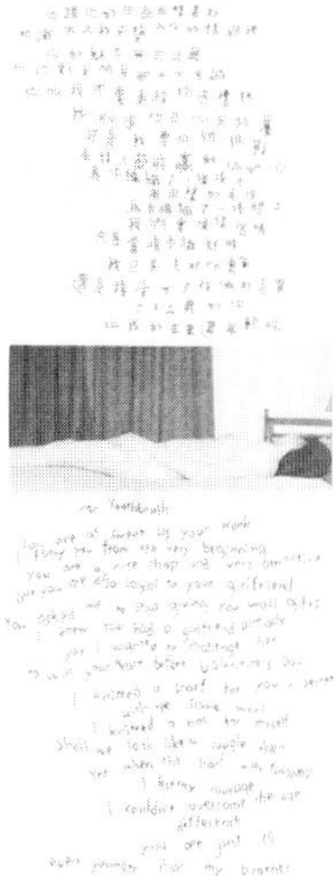

MR WISE

I admired you and your work
knowledgeable,
sincere,
simple,
dignified

Whenever I was stuck with my work
you gave me insights
encouraged me to explore another possibility
the way for alternatives

I liked your smile
I liked the way you looked at me
just like Mr Playboy

The meaning behind your work was so rich
the power underneath was so great
that's what I wanted to achieve one day

Though you might not be as famous
as Piccasso
you were my great tutor
my great tutor indeed

黃美玉

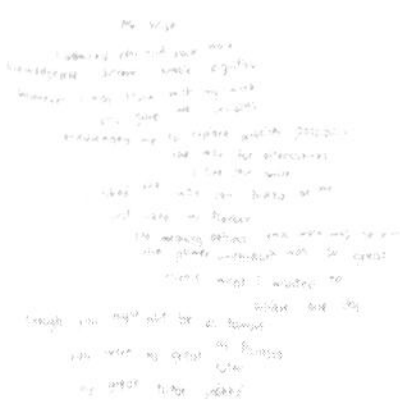

智慧先生

我欣賞你和你的作品
知識豐富
誠眞
簡潔
尊重

當我煩惱不知如何創作
你給我亮光
使我敢於開拓其他可能
另覓出路

我喜歡你的笑容
你凝望我的眼神
令我想起那個花花公子

你的作品意念豐富
內裡隱藏著無比的力量
盼望我的作品也有這一天的功力

你的名氣
未必如畢加索
但你是我的導師
偉大的導航者

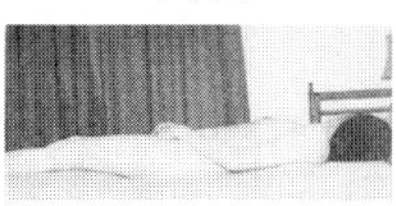

MR CARNATION

Who has ever annoyed me
and made me cry so much?
it's you and it hurts

I was so scared to show my fancy to you
by giving you a birthday gift which I made
for how many days and nights

In return,
you refused me in a very sophisticated way
you were **afraid** that I liked you too much
you could not tell me why you felt it wouldn't work
and I could not explain either why I liked you so much

I controlled my tears before you
then, I could control it no more
tears dropped naturally when I sat down on the train alone
I still wore my sunglasses even though it was at night,
trying to hide my sadness in front of strangers

We went to see an exhibition, to have a meal, to dance,
to exchange emails and greeting cards …
and most of all you bought my paintings!
but all became nothing and meaningless

Surely, I'll channel my emotions
to my work
to my friends and family
but not you anymore
I don't want to scare you and to be hurt again.

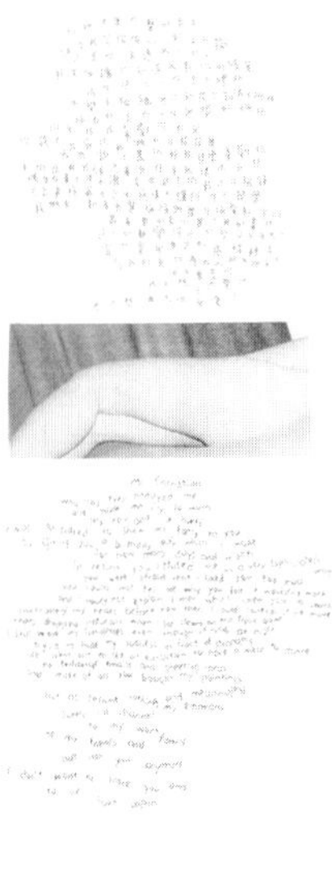

給她送康乃馨的男子

誰令我苦惱煩心
哭泣不斷？
正是你
傷透我心的人

我害怕讓你知道我對你的傾慕
爲你送上一份生日禮物
用雙手編織
也不知花了多少個日與夜

換來的
是你十分細膩的婉拒
你害怕我喜歡你太深
你說不出爲何我們不可能發展
我也說不盡何解我這麼喜歡你

在你面前我強忍著淚
往後我情不自禁
獨自在車上淚水湧流
夜深了仍戴上太陽鏡
只是要隱藏自己的感情不讓陌生人發覺

我們曾一起看展覽、晚膳、跳舞、交換電郵賀咭
最重要的是你買了我的畫作！
這一切都變得不打緊，沒有意思了

我當然會把自己的感情轉易
爲我的創作
爲我的朋友與家人
但不會是你
我不想令你驚恐
也不想再爲你受傷了

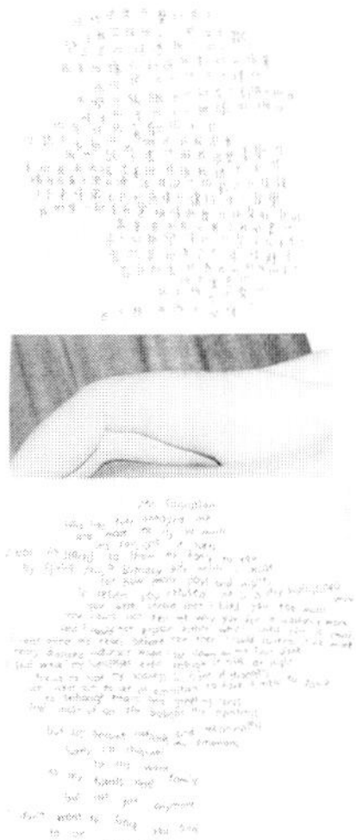

MR ADMIRER

The feeling of being admired in secret
is so good
and wonderful

I admire a couple of nice chaps
but none of them
respond the way that I hope

Those viewers admired my work
then
there was one who
asked me to go for a drink

I was very positive
why not
to have a new friend
an admirer

to have more choices
certainly I'll tell Mr Carnation
somebody's interested
in me

at least I can see how he reacts
make him **jealous**
yeah, if he really likes me
he should be more aggressive

Being a stranger
the way you looked at me
there's something more inside your eyes
adoration of my work and me

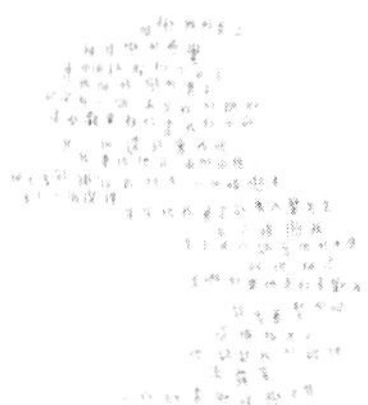

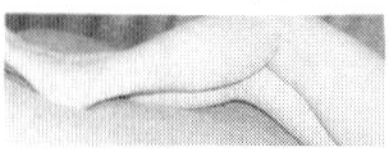

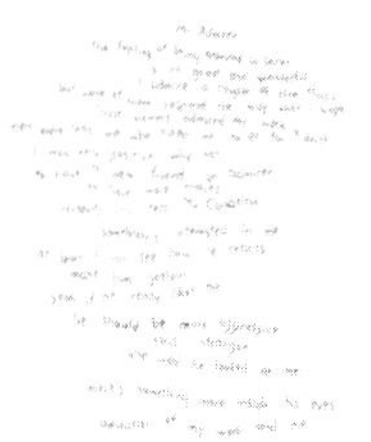

暗戀我的男子

被暗戀的感覺
眞的很舒服
妙不可言

我所暗戀的男子
卻沒有一個
滿足我的期盼

這些觀眾
都欣賞我的作品
其中一位
還約會我呢！

我要給他正面的回應
何不
多認識一位新朋友
一位暗戀者

多了一個選擇
肯定地
我會告訴康乃馨先生
有人暗戀我

至少可以試出他的反應
叫他妒忌
是啊，如果他眞的喜歡我
該多著緊些呢！

陌生人啊
你凝望我的眼神
流露著
一份欣賞與暗戀之情

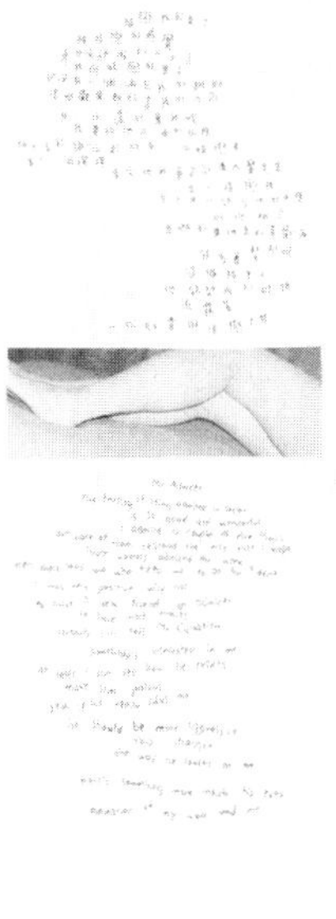

MR GENEROUS

You were so nice to me
I liked you a lot indeed
but you were too young for me
I wanted you to be **30 something**
right now!

You had given me a lot of gifts
very generous
very thoughtful
your behaviour was very mature
for your age

Thanks for walking with me
along the River Thames
hand in hand
even though we were not a couple
but very close friends

You're going to make a model
a reflection of me
through your eyes
how will it be?

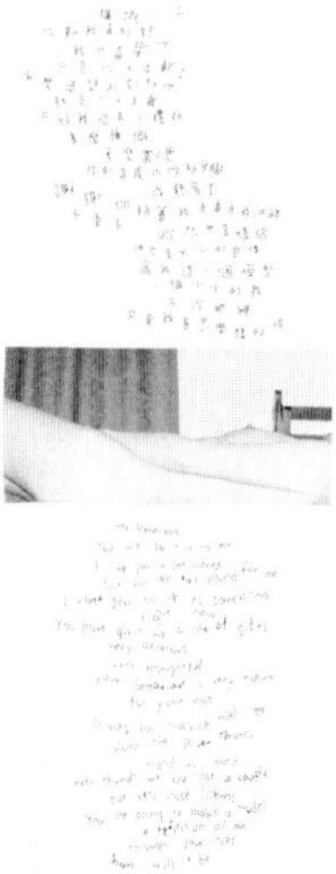

慷慨小子

你對我眞的好
我也喜歡你
只是你太年輕了
多麼渴望此刻的你
就是三十多歲！

你給我很多小禮物
多麼慷慨
多麼富心思
你的表現比你的年齡
成熟多了

謝謝你陪著我走
泰吾時河畔
手牽手
縱然不是情侶
但也是交心的良伴

爲我造一個模型
一個小小的我
在你眼裡
究竟我是怎麼樣的呢？

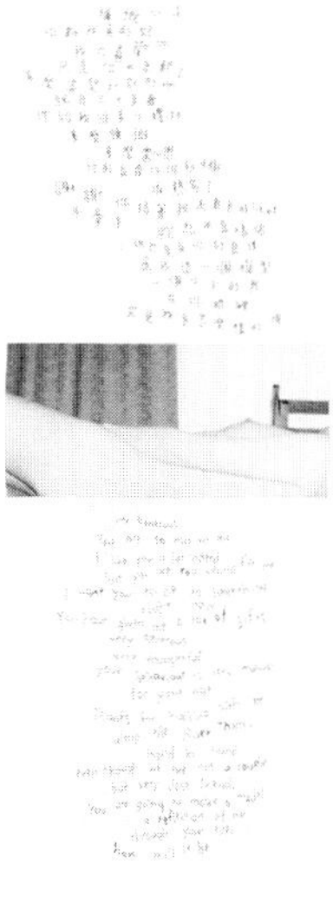

HOW CAN I FALL IN LOVE WITH A DEAD YOUNG MAN?

Her beloved son
handsome but dying **too** young
the more I get to know your story
the deeper is my feeling towards you
but in secret
how can I tell anybody I fell in love with a dead man?

How can it be?
we never met
just by seeing your picture
I fall in love with you
how can I put it into words
so attractive
not just because of your sweetness and gentleness
but the persona within your heart and exposed on your face

How could anyone dare to take your life
was it the storm?
such a mystery
who can bear to lose a handsome young man
like you
beloved by your parents and sister
befriended by the people around you

I can't resist
the temptation
to get a copy of your picture
but …
will it upset your poor mother?

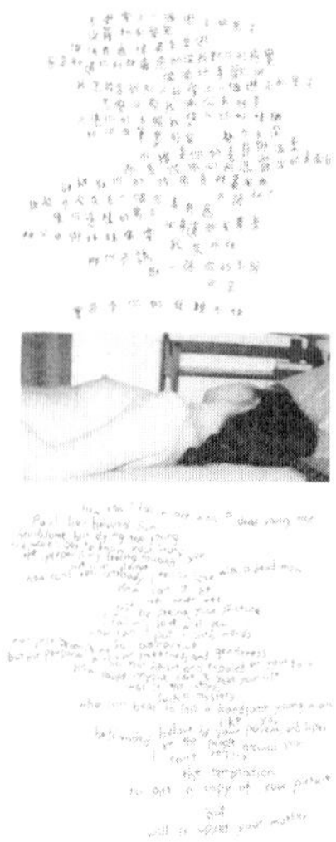

(In *Forces of Destiny* by *Poetry Now*, p.10, 2001)

怎麼愛上一個逝去的男子

她的愛兒
俊俏有為，可惜英年早逝

愈是知道你的故事
愈加深我對你的感覺
偷偷地喜歡你
我怎能告訴別人我愛上一個逝去的男子？

怎麼可能？
我倆從未相見
只憑你的玉照
我墮入你的情網
如何用筆墨形容
魅力太深
不獨是你的善良與溫柔
而是從你心內流露出的真面孔

誰敢取你的性命
是那暴風雨？
太詭秘了
誰能忍受失去一個年青有為
像你這樣的男子
被父母與妹妹痛愛
受身邊朋友尊崇

我奈不住
那份引誘
取一張你的玉照
可是
會否令你的母親不快？

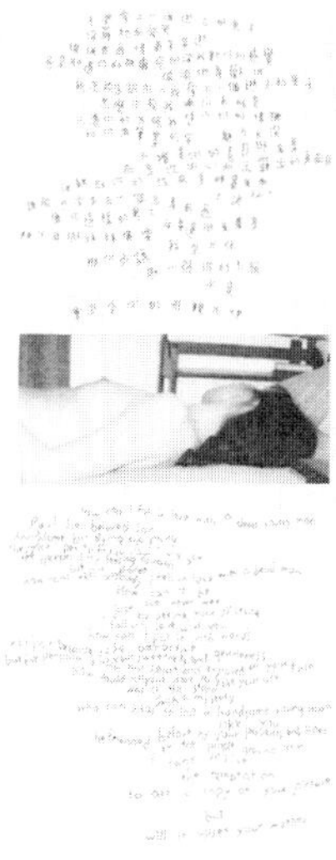

MISS GREEN & MISS RED

I never thought I would fall in love with a woman
Only twice
and just for a very short moment

I was lying on the sofa
Miss Green was sitting next to me
suddenly, I was attracted to her
I wanted to touch her body
but the emotion didn't last for long
maybe just a few minutes
or even a few seconds ...

The other time was similar
I was talking with Miss Red after the service
she was wearing a red jacket
it was as red as her face
she had very thin skin
she was chatting with me
and I had the feeling for her
she looked so charming.
Again
it didn't last long ...

Once I was arguing with Mr Handsome
he disagreed very much on gay issues
I was very critical too
it was impossible to have any consensus
finally
I challenged him
what do you fall in love with?
a person or her/his sex organ!
so, why do we bother so much about their sexuality
but not their personality?

Though I'm still straight at the moment.
I always remind myself to be open
and respect other people's different
sexual orientation.

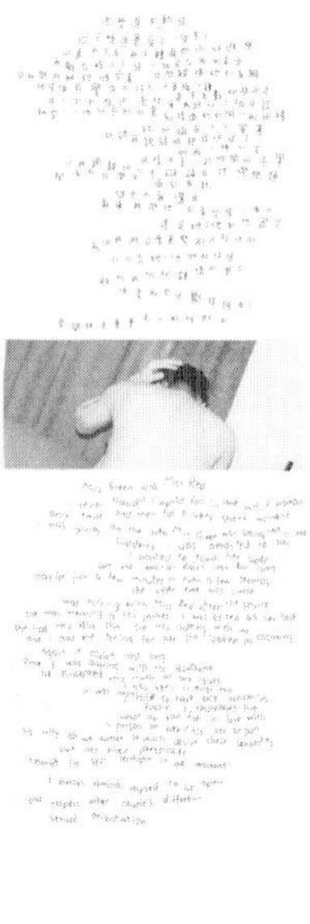

怎麼爲女人動情

從沒想過會愛上一個女人
印象中只有兩次
轉瞬即逝的遐想

我躺在椅子上
綠小姐坐在我的身旁
突然間我被她吸引著
很想觸摸她的身軀
但這個感覺並不持久
只是幾分鐘
甚至是數秒間而已

另一次也相近
崇拜後我跟紅小姐交談
她穿了一件紅色的外套
紅得像她的臉一般明媚
她的臉皮十分單薄
她跟我說話時把我迷住了
叫我心神不定
同樣
又是一剎那間的感覺

一次我跟靚仔小生
辯論同性戀問題
鬧得不可開交
面紅耳熱
誰也不肯讓步
最後，我問他：
究竟你愛一個人
還是她／他的性器官！
眞的
爲何我們這麼著緊別人的性向
而不是她／他們的性情

雖然我仍然鍾情於男子
但是我也不斷提醒自己
要開放及尊重別人的性取向

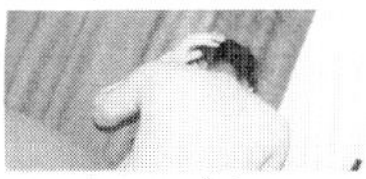

MR PRIDE

Why were you so quiet
you seemed to bear the burden of
the whole nation
or even of the whole world
were you the Messiah?

Why couldn't you enjoy the happiness
being with the pretty woman
why were you so stupid?
were you gay?

Were you too proud to express
your true feeling for the woman
you loved so deeply in heart
for such a long time

The prides and prejudices
avoided you to love
openly
with your freewill

Yet,
you were brave enough
to sort out
what you had done wrongly

A man can correct his fault
by doing something good for others
even in a secret manner

No wonder at the end
you won her love gradually
in fact
I'm longing for such a real man too

眞漢子

為何你這樣沉默
好像背負了一國的重擔
甚至是全世界的包袱
你是彌賽亞？

為何你不能享受
與漂亮的女子在一起
你愚不可及
還是男同志？

你的傲慢難於啓齒
內心眞情
為這女子
深深地愛著
久久地等待

傲慢與偏見
攔阻你
公開地
自由地宣愛

然而
你勇敢地
尋求辦法
承認一己的錯失

一個能為自己悔過的男子
主動為他人做一些補救功夫
甚至不為人道

怪不得到最終
你還是漸漸地贏取了她的心
其實
我也在追尋這樣的眞漢子

MR HOMELESS

Almost every time I went to the library
you stood in front of the entrance
selling *Big Issues* for a living

What's the difference between you and me
we both worked very hard
I wondered how many copies did you sell
for standing 7 hours a day both in Summer and in Winter

Where did you live
did you have any education
did you have another job
what made you become homeless?

I didn't know your name
I just said hi or good morning to you
and you said hi or smiled to me too

Did I want to know you more in person
not just one of the homeless
suddenly I recognised you had blue eyes
was I attracted to you

How could it be?
you had no job, no place to live, no money,
you had nothing
yet you looked a nice person
with sweet personality from within your heart

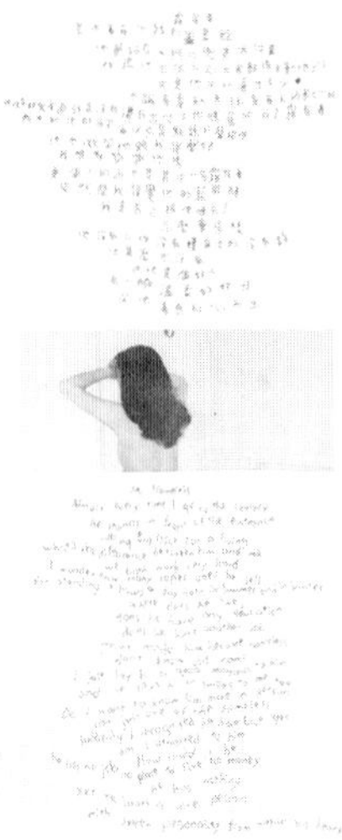

露宿者

差不多每次我到圖書館
你都站在大門口
兜售＜大件事＞

我跟你有何分別
大家都很辛勤地工作
究竟你可以賣出多少本
不論春夏秋冬就是每天站著七小時

你住在那兒
受過教育沒有
還有其他工作嗎
爲何成了露宿者

我不知你的名字
每次只是點頭打聲招呼
你也微笑地跟我說聲好

我想多認識你嗎
更個人的
而不是其中一名露宿者

突然間
我發覺你的藍眼睛
我是否已被你吸引了
怎麼會這樣

你沒有工作
沒有棲身之所
沒有錢
你甚麼也沒有

但你是個好人
有一臉溫柔的性情
從你善良的心而出

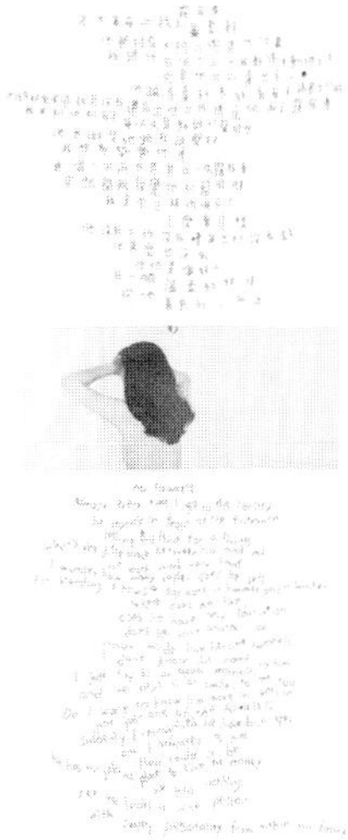

BLUE EYES

I love the man with blue eyes
I like blue eyes and blue eyes only

My man
my husband
my partner …
it doesn't matter how to call him

I don't mind if my man
is a divorcee,
a widower,
a builder,
a non-Christian …
but he must love me truly
with honesty
just like a **transparent** vase

I want to have a child,
and his name will be Hugo
too old for a first baby?
I wish to adopt one

Too many children are waiting for
a big hug,
an unconditional love,
a warm and safe home
why bother to have my own baby!

I'll be contented
if he agrees to adopt a child
or bring me one
have a blue-eyed man and get a child for free!

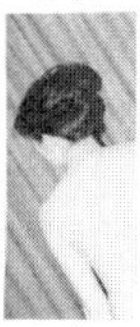

藍眼睛

我愛藍眼睛的男子
我只愛藍眼睛的他

我的男人
我的丈夫
我的伴侶
怎樣稱呼他也不相干，也不打緊

不介意我的男人
離了婚
或已喪偶
或是裝修工人
甚至是非基督徒
但他必然要誠懇地愛我
全心全意
好像透明的花瓶般真摯

我想有一個孩子
爲他命名叫雨果
不宜當高齡產婦？
但我可收養一個孩子

這麼多的孤兒期待著
擁抱
無條件的愛
溫暖又安全的家
何解偏偏要自己生的孩子！

我會心滿意足
如果他同意收養一個孩子
或是給我帶來一個
愛一個藍眼睛的男人
育一個收養的孩子